QUICK MEALS

Michelle Berriedale Johnson

HAMLYN

CONTENTS

This edition prepared under the supervision of
Joanna Morris

This edition published in 1990 by
The Hamlyn Publishing Group Limited,
a division of the Octopus Publishing Group,
Michelin House, 81 Fulham Road,
London SW3 6RB

© 1980 Cathay Books

ISBN 0 600 56996 9

Produced by Mandarin Offset
Printed and Bound in Hong Kong

INTRODUCTION

Here's a cookbook designed especially for those who enjoy good food but whose busy life styles leave them limited time for cooking. It's a book for active families, for working couples, for singles who like to entertain with flair.

The recipes are geared to suit every occasion and everyone's pocket. You'll find a Steak au Poivre for a special celebration as well as a protein-punched omelet for the day before payday. Whatever your choice, the taste is right. And although we've used some time-saving convenience foods here and there, the taste is usually fresh.

While no recipe in this book should take more than 45 minutes to prepare—and many take far, far less—it's organization that will tell in the long run. Analyze the recipes for the most efficient order of preparation...equip yourself with the right tools, such as good knives and a garlic press...and go to it! In less than an hour, a delicious meal will be yours.

NOTES:

Always preheat the oven to the specified temperature.

Margarine can be substituted for butter in all recipes.

If substituting dried herbs for fresh, use a third of the amount;
if substituting fresh for dried, use 3 times the amount.

APPETIZERS

Creamed Mushrooms on Toast

4 tablespoons butter
1 small onion, finely chopped
Juice of 1 lemon
½ lb mushrooms, sliced
4 teaspoons cornstarch
½ teaspoon curry powder
1½ cups light cream
Salt and pepper
4 slices hot toast

Melt the butter in a skillet. Add the onion and sauté until soft. Add the lemon juice and mushrooms and sauté for 3 minutes.

Stir in the cornstarch and curry powder and cook, stirring, for 2 minutes. Gradually add the cream and cook gently until thickened. Season to taste with salt and pepper.

Spoon the mixture over the toast. Garnish with parsley if desired.
4 servings

Caviar-Stuffed Tomatoes

3 tablespoons butter
1 small onion, finely
  chopped
1 cup soft bread
  crumbs
1 jar (3½ oz) red
  lumpfish caviar
Grated rind of
  ½ lemon
Salt and pepper
Cayenne pepper
4 large tomatoes,
  halved and seeded
2 to 3 tablespoons
  dry white wine

Melt 2 tablespoons of the butter in a skillet. Add the onion and sauté until soft. Add the bread crumbs and cook until golden. Set aside 4 teaspoons of the crumbs.

Stir the caviar into the remaining bread crumbs. Add the lemon rind; season with salt, pepper and cayenne.

Fill the tomatoes with the caviar mixture. Spoon the wine over the filling. Sprinkle with the reserved bread crumbs and dot with the remaining butter.

Bake in a preheated 350° oven for 15 to 20 minutes, or until the tomatoes are just tender.

4 servings

Artichoke and Ham Salad

2 cans (14 oz each)
  artichoke hearts,
  drained
¼ cup Italian salad
  dressing
4 slices cooked ham
1 tablespoon butter

Toss the artichoke hearts with the salad dressing and arrange on a shallow serving dish.

Cut the ham into strips. Melt the butter in a skillet and add the ham. Cook until lightly browned; drain.

Sprinkle the ham over the artichoke hearts and serve at once.

8 servings

NOTE: For a heartier salad, sauté sliced mushrooms with the ham.

Avocado Waldorf

2 pears, cubed
2 tablespoons lemon
 juice
8 large pitted ripe
 olives
1½ tablespoons
 mayonnaise
Salt and pepper
2 avocados, halved
 and pitted

Toss the pears with some of the lemon juice to prevent discoloration.

Halve two of the olives for garnish, if desired, and chop the remainder.

Combine the mayonnaise and the remaining lemon juice in a bowl. Add the pears, chopped olives and salt and pepper to taste.

Mound the salad mixture in the avocado halves and garnish each with an olive half. Sprinkle with chopped nuts if desired.

4 servings

Anchovy Melon Salad

1 medium melon,
 halved and seeded
1 can (2 oz) anchovy
 fillets
Juice of 1 lemon
Juice of 1 orange

Scoop out the melon flesh using a melon baller (or peel and cut into cubes); place in a serving dish.

Drain the anchovy fillets, reserving 1 tablespoon of the oil, and add to the melon.

Combine the lemon and orange juices with the reserved oil and pour over the salad; toss gently. Chill before serving. Garnish with a sprig of watercress if desired.

4 servings

Eggs Mimosa

4 hard-cooked eggs
1 jar (2 oz) red or
    black lumpfish
    caviar
1 tablespoon lemon
    juice
6 to 8 tablespoons
    mayonnaise

Halve the eggs lengthwise, remove the yolks and place the whites on a serving platter. Fill the whites with the caviar.

Press the yolks through a sieve and spoon them over the caviar, reserving 1 tablespoon for the garnish, if desired.

Combine the lemon juice and mayonnaise and spoon over the filled eggs, covering them completely. Garnish with sieved egg yolk and lettuce leaves if desired.

4 servings

NOTE: For a flavorful variation, combine finely chopped onion with the caviar before filling the egg whites. Add some color to the dish by sprinkling red or black caviar over the sieved egg yolk garnish.

Shrimp-Stuffed Cucumbers

1 large cucumber
1 package (3 oz)
    cream cheese,
    softened
2 tablespoons lemon
    juice
1 package (5 oz)
    frozen cooked and
    peeled shrimp
1 jar (4 oz) chopped
    pimientos,
    drained
2 tablespoons
    chopped mint
Salt and pepper

Cut the cucumber crosswise into 8 sections. Hollow out the center of each section to form cups; stand them upright on a serving dish.

Combine the cream cheese and lemon juice. Reserve 8 shrimp for garnish and chop the remainder. Add to the cream cheese mixture with the pimientos and mint. Season with salt and pepper to taste; mix well.

Spoon the filling into the cucumber cups and garnish with the reserved shrimp.

4 servings

Asparagus Gratinée

4 slices pumper-
  nickel toast,
  buttered
1 can (15 oz)
  asparagus spears,
  drained
½ cup shredded
  Swiss cheese
Pepper

Place the toast on a broiler pan. Arrange the asparagus spears on the toast and sprinkle with the cheese.

Place under a preheated broiler and cook until the cheese is melted and lightly browned, about 4 minutes. Sprinkle with pepper to taste and serve hot.

4 servings

MAIN COURSES

Pork Chops with Mustard Sauce

2 tablespoons butter
1 onion, thinly sliced
2 tablespoons flour
Salt and pepper
4 loin pork chops
½ cup dry sherry
¼ cup chicken broth
2 tablespoons Dijon
  mustard

Melt the butter in a skillet. Add the onion and sauté until soft. Remove with a slotted spoon and set aside.

Season the flour with salt and pepper and use to coat the chops. Add them to the skillet and brown quickly on both sides.

Return the onion to the skillet and add the sherry and broth. Cover and simmer until the chops are tender, about 30 minutes.

Place the chops on a warm serving dish. Add the mustard to the sauce in the skillet and stir well to combine. Season if necessary. Pour the sauce over the chops and serve.

4 servings

Pork with Plums

2 tablespoons flour
Salt and pepper
1 to 1½ lb pork
    tenderloin, cut
    into 4 pieces
4 tablespoons butter
1 can (16 oz) plums,
    drained and pitted
¼ teaspoon ground
    cinnamon
⅔ cup dry red wine

Season the flour with the salt and pepper and use to coat the pork.

Melt the butter in a large skillet or flameproof casserole. Add the pork and lightly brown on both sides.

Mash the plums in a bowl. Stir in the cinnamon and wine and pour the mixture over the pork. Cover and simmer 30 minutes.

Serve hot, garnished with chopped parsley if desired.

4 servings

Barbecued Spareribs

2 lb pork spareribs
SAUCE:
5 tablespoons catsup
2 tablespoons honey
3 tablespoons soy
  sauce
3 tablespoons red
  wine vinegar
1 tablespoon tomato
  paste
½ teaspoon salt
1 cup beef broth

Place the spareribs in a large pot of boiling salted water. Cook for 10 to 12 minutes, skimming occasionally. Meanwhile, combine the sauce ingredients in a bowl.

Drain the spareribs well and let cool slightly. Place them in a large shallow roasting pan and generously coat with the sauce. Bake in a preheated 375° oven, brushing the ribs with the sauce several times, until cooked through, about 35 minutes.

Place the spareribs on a warm serving dish. Place the roasting pan over moderate heat and add any remaining sauce. Bring to a boil and cook until the sauce is well reduced and thickened. Serve the sauce separately and follow the meat with a hearty salad, such as Tuscan Bean Salad (page 61).
4 servings

Frank and Bean Stew

2 tablespoons butter
1 large onion,
   chopped
4 frankfurters, sliced
¼ lb garlic sausage,
   sliced
1 tablespoon capers
2 cans (16 oz each)
   red kidney beans,
   drained
⅔ cup chicken broth
2 slices bacon,
   cooked and
   crumbled
Salt and pepper
2 tablespoons
   chopped parsley

Melt the butter in a flameproof casserole. Add the onion and sauté until soft. Add the frankfurters, sausage, capers and beans; mix well.

Stir in the broth and bacon. Cover and bake in a preheated 350° oven for 30 minutes.

Add salt and pepper to taste and stir in the parsley. Serve hot with crusty French bread.

4 servings

NOTE: Round out this dish with a vegetable salad and end the meal with a fruit dessert.

Orange-Glazed Ham

6 ham steaks, about
¼-inch thick

GLAZE:

2 teaspoons Dijon
mustard

⅔ cup orange juice

2 tablespoons brown
sugar

Grated rind of
1 orange

½ teaspoon ground
cloves

Arrange the ham steaks in a large shallow broiler pan. Combine the glaze ingredients in a saucepan and bring to a boil. Simmer for 5 minutes and set aside to cool slightly. Brush the glaze over both sides of the ham steaks. If time permits, set aside to marinate for 20 to 30 minutes.

Place the pan under a preheated broiler and cook for 5 to 7 minutes on each side, basting occasionally with the remaining glaze.

Transfer to serving plates and spoon the pan juices over the steaks. Garnish with orange slices and fresh herbs if desired.

6 servings

Veal Cutlets with Sour Cream

3 tablespoons flour
Salt and pepper
1 lb veal scallops
4 tablespoons butter
1 small onion, finely
chopped
2 tablespoons capers,
undrained
5 tablespoons sour
cream

Season half the flour with salt and pepper and use to coat the veal.

Melt half the butter in a skillet. Add the veal and sauté until tender and golden, about 5 minutes on each side. Remove and set aside.

Melt the remaining butter in the skillet. Add the onion and sauté until soft. Add the remaining flour and cook, stirring, for 1 to 2 minutes.

Add the capers and their vinegar along with 1 cup water. Cook, stirring, until the sauce thickens. Stir in the sour cream. Return the veal to the skillet and heat through. Sprinkle with chopped parsley, if desired, and serve with hot rice.

4 servings

Green Peppercorn Steak

2 beef sirloin or filet
  steaks (5 oz each)
Salt
2 tablespoons green
  peppercorns,
  drained
1 tablespoon
  chopped thyme
1 tablespoon butter
1 clove garlic,
  crushed
¼ lb mushrooms,
  sliced
½ cup dry red wine
2 green onions,
  chopped
1 teaspoon Dijon
  mustard
Worcestershire
  sauce

Season the steaks with salt. Press in
the peppercorns and thyme.

Melt the butter in a skillet and sauté
the steaks 2 to 4 minutes on each side,
or until cooked to the desired degree of
doneness.

Meanwhile, in a saucepan, bring the
garlic, mushrooms and wine to a boil.
Cook rapidly until reduced and thickened. Stir in the green onions, mustard
and a dash of the Worcestershire.

Arrange the steaks on a warm serving dish and spoon the sauce over
them. Serve at once, garnished with
thyme if desired.

2 servings

NOTE: For a variation on this sauce,
add a tablespoon of sherry vinegar
when you add the mustard.

Steak au Poivre

1 to 2 tablespoons
  peppercorns,
  crushed
4 eye round or
  cubed beef steaks
4 tablespoons butter
2 tablespoons
  brandy, warmed
1 cup light cream
Salt

Press the peppercorns into both sides of the steaks. Set aside for 15 minutes.

Melt the butter in a heavy skillet and sauté the steaks quickly for 2 minutes on each side. Lower the heat and cook to the desired degree of doneness, 3 to 7 minutes per side. Transfer to a warm serving dish and keep warm.

Add the brandy to the skillet and ignite. When the flames subside, stir in the cream. Cook briskly for 2 minutes, stirring constantly. Season with salt to taste. Pour the sauce over the steaks or serve separately.

4 servings

NOTE: If available, use green peppercorns instead of black for a more subtle flavor.

Ground Beef Kabobs, Indian Style

1½ lb ground beef
1 small onion, minced
2 cloves garlic, minced
1 tablespoon tomato paste
Juice of ½ lemon or 1 lime
1 tablespoon flour
½ teaspoon each ground cumin, chili powder and coriander
Pinch each of ground cinnamon, ginger, nutmeg and cloves
Salt and pepper

Combine the beef, onion, garlic, tomato paste, lemon juice and flour in a bowl; mix well. Mix in the spices and season with salt and pepper. Mix again. (The mixture should be fairly smooth.)

Divide the mixture into 6 portions and form into sausage shapes around skewers. Place in the freezer just long enough to firm up.

Cook the kabobs under a preheated broiler, turning occasionally, until well browned, 15 to 20 minutes.

For a special occasion, place the kabobs on a bed of shredded lettuce and garnish with lemon and cucumber slices and mint. Serve hot with rice.

6 servings

NOTE: Ground lamb or veal may be substituted for the beef.

Chili con Carne

4 tablespoons butter
2 large onions, finely
  chopped
2 cloves garlic,
  crushed
1 lb lean ground beef
2 teaspoons chili
  powder
4 teaspoons ground
  cumin
¼ cup tomato paste
2 cans (16 oz each)
  red kidney beans,
  drained
1¼ cups beef broth
Salt and pepper

Melt the butter in a flameproof casserole. Add the onions and garlic and sauté until golden. Stir in the beef and cook, stirring, for 10 minutes. Pour off the excess fat.

Stir the chili powder, cumin and tomato paste into the beef. Add the beans, broth and salt and pepper to taste. Cover and cook in a preheated 350° oven for 25 minutes.

Sprinkle with chopped parsley if desired. Serve hot, with hot cooked rice, cooked macaroni or crusty French bread.

4 servings

Beef Stroganoff

2 tablespoons butter
2 onions, sliced
1 to 2 cloves garlic, crushed
1½ lb beef rump or sirloin steak
2 tablespoons dry red wine
¼ lb mushrooms, sliced
1 teaspoon Dijon mustard
¾ cup sour cream
Salt and pepper
1 tablespoon chopped thyme
1 tablespoon chopped parsley

Melt the butter in a large skillet. Add the onions and garlic and sauté until lightly browned.

Cut the steak into thin strips. Add it to the skillet and brown on all sides. Add the wine and boil until the liquid is reduced, about 5 minutes. Add the mushrooms, mustard, sour cream and salt and pepper to taste; simmer for 5 minutes.

Stir in the thyme and parsley and serve with noodles.

4 servings

NOTE: A tablespoon or two of brandy can make this dish more flavorful.

Lamb Chops with Sherry Sauce

8 loin lamb chops
1 clove garlic, slivered
1 to 2 tablespoons oil
2 tablespoons butter
1 tablespoon each chopped thyme, parsley, sage and chives
⅔ cup dry sherry
½ cup heavy cream
Salt and pepper

Cut small slits in the chops and push in the slivered garlic.

Warm the oil and butter in a heavy skillet. Add the chops and brown on both sides. Reduce the heat and cook for 4 to 6 minutes on each side, until the chops are cooked through. Drain the chops on paper towels and transfer to a warm serving dish.

Add the herbs and sherry to the skillet and boil rapidly until thick, about 2 minutes. Stir in the cream and salt and pepper to taste. Cook until reduced slightly and thickened.

Spoon the sauce over the chops or serve separately. Garnish with finely chopped parsley if desired.

4 servings

Chicken Kabobs

6 boned and skinned
  chicken breast
  halves
1 teaspoon Dijon
  mustard
¼ cup olive oil
2 tablespoons lemon
  juice
1 clove garlic, sliced
1 teaspoon dried
  mixed herbs
Salt and pepper
6 slices bacon,
  halved
Sage sprigs

Cut the chicken into 1½-inch cubes. Combine the mustard, oil, lemon juice and garlic in a bowl. Stir in the herbs and season to taste with salt and pepper. Add the chicken, stir well and set aside to marinate for 20 minutes.

Roll up the bacon pieces. Thread the chicken chunks and bacon alternately on 6 skewers, interspersing with sage leaves to taste. Cook under a preheated broiler, spooning the marinade over the kabobs from time to time, until golden and tender, 5 to 7 minutes on each side.

Garnish, if desired, with lemon slices and sage and serve hot with buttered noodles and a green salad or vegetable.

6 servings

Chili Chicken Livers

1 tablespoon oil
1 large onion, thinly sliced
2 cloves garlic, crushed
1 can (14 oz) tomatoes
1 tablespoon tomato paste
1 teaspoon dried mixed herbs
1 to 2 teaspoons chili powder
1 hot chile pepper, seeded and chopped
Salt and pepper
¾ lb chicken livers, coarsely chopped
1 tablespoon flour
2 tablespoons butter
¼ lb mushrooms, sliced
⅔ cup dry white wine

Heat the oil in a saucepan. Add the onion and garlic and cook until soft but not browned, about 5 minutes. Stir in the tomatoes with their juice and bring to a boil. Cook rapidly for 5 minutes. Stir in the tomato paste, herbs, chili powder, chile pepper and salt and pepper to taste. Return to a boil and cook, uncovered, for 20 minutes.

Dredge the chicken livers in the flour. Melt the butter in a skillet and add the livers. Sauté until lightly browned, about 5 minutes. Drain on paper towels and add to the tomato sauce along with the mushrooms and wine. Bring to a boil and cook rapidly until thickened, 5 to 7 minutes.

Taste for seasoning and serve with noodles or rice.

4 to 6 servings

Chef's Salad

½ lb spinach
¼ lb Gruyère cheese, thinly sliced
¼ lb cooked chicken breast
¼ lb cooked ham
¼ lb roast beef
1 tomato, sliced
2 hard-cooked eggs, sliced
Stuffed olives, halved
Chopped basil leaves
1 tablespoon chopped parsley
DRESSING:
2 tablespoons lemon juice
¼ cup olive oil
1 teaspoon Dijon mustard
1 teaspoon honey
2 teaspoons chopped thyme
2 tablespoons chopped nuts
Salt and pepper

Tear the spinach into small bits and arrange on a plate or in a bowl.

Cut the cheese, chicken, ham, and beef into 2-inch strips and arrange in sections on top of the spinach.

Arrange the tomato and egg slices and the olives over the meat. Sprinkle with basil and parsley.

Mix all the dressing ingredients together, seasoning with salt and pepper to taste. Spoon the dressing over the salad and serve at once.

4 servings

NOTE: A chef's salad is the perfect opportunity to use any leftover ingredients in your refrigerator. Look for pimientos, ripe olives, carrots, peas and celery.

Chicken Salad with Green Grapes

1 clove garlic,
   crushed
4 green onions,
   chopped
½ cup mayonnaise
Pinch of paprika
1 teaspoon curry
   powder
1 tablespoon minced
   stuffed olives
Worcestershire
   sauce
Hot pepper sauce
Salt and pepper
1 cup walnuts,
   coarsely chopped
¼ lb seedless green
   grapes, halved
1 lb cooked chicken
   breast, shredded
2 tablespoons
   chopped fresh
   tarragon
Lettuce leaves
Whole green grapes
Tarragon sprigs

In a bowl, combine the garlic, onions, mayonnaise, paprika and curry powder; mix well. Stir in the olives and a dash each of Worcestershire and hot pepper sauce. Season to taste with salt and pepper. Cover and set aside to allow the flavors to mingle.

In a bowl, combine the walnuts, grape halves and chicken. Add the chopped tarragon and stir well. Pour on the dressing and toss well.

Arrange the lettuce leaves in a salad bowl or plate. Spoon the chicken salad on top. Chill until serving time. Garnish with grapes and tarragon sprigs if desired.

4 to 6 servings

Pineapple Chicken

1 chicken (3 lb), cut up
1 onion, thinly sliced
1 teaspoon salt
¼ teaspoon pepper
½ teaspoon dried rosemary
½ teaspoon ground ginger
Pinch of paprika
3 cans (6 oz each) unsweetened pineapple juice
Chopped parsley

Place the chicken in a casserole. Sprinkle with onion, salt, pepper, rosemary, ginger and paprika. Pour the pineapple juice over all.

Bake in a preheated 350° oven until the chicken is cooked and browned on top, about 45 minutes. Serve hot, garnished with chopped parsley.

4 servings

NOTE: Try substituting pear or apricot nectar for the pineapple juice.

Chicken and Walnut Salad

2 cups diced cooked
  chicken
2 stalks celery,
  coarsely chopped
1 large apple, diced
½ cup coarsely
  chopped walnuts
6 tablespoons
  mayonnaise
1 to 2 tablespoons
  light cream
  (optional)

Combine the chicken, celery, apple and walnuts in a large bowl.

If necessary, thin the mayonnaise with the light cream until it is the consistency of heavy cream. (Refrigerate if not serving immediately.)

Pour the sauce over the chicken and toss gently until all the ingredients are well coated.

Spoon into a serving dish. Serve chilled or at room temperature, garnished with watercress or celery leaves if desired.

4 servings

Seafood Curry

2 onions
½ sweet red pepper
2 stalks celery
2 tablespoons oil
½ cup sliced
   mushrooms
1½ tablespoons
   curry powder
½ teaspoon each
   turmeric and
   ginger
1 apple, diced
½ lb haddock fillet,
   cut into chunks
¼ lb shrimp, peeled
   and deveined
½ cup raisins
1 teaspoon
   Worcestershire
   sauce
2 teaspoons tomato
   paste
⅓ cup white wine
Salt and pepper
2 tablespoons plain
   yogurt
Juice of ½ lemon

Chop the onions, red pepper and celery. Heat the oil in a large skillet. Add the chopped vegetables and sliced mushrooms; sauté for 5 minutes. Add the curry powder, turmeric and ginger and cook, stirring, for about 2 minutes.

Add the apple, haddock, shrimp, raisins, Worcestershire and tomato paste; stir well. Stir in the wine and ¼ cup water. Season to taste with salt and pepper. Cover and simmer gently until heated throughout, about 10 minutes.

Just before serving, stir in the yogurt and lemon juice. Serve with hot rice.
4 servings

Fish and Eggs Mornay

4 smoked white fish
    fillets (about 1 lb)
2 cups milk
1 bay leaf
4 eggs
3 tablespoons butter
6 tablespoons flour
¾ cup shredded
    Cheddar cheese
Pepper

Place the fish fillets in a large skillet with the milk and bay leaf. Poach over low heat until tender, about 10 minutes. Using a slotted spatula, arrange the fillets in a flameproof dish and keep warm. Strain the milk and reserve; discard the bay leaf.

Poach the eggs in simmering water for 2 to 3 minutes. Meanwhile, melt the butter in a saucepan. Add the flour and cook, stirring, for 2 minutes. Stir in the milk and cook, stirring, until thickened. Stir in ½ cup of the cheese.

Using a slotted spoon, place a poached egg on each fillet. Top with the cheese sauce and sprinkle with the remaining ¼ cup cheese and the pepper. Cook under a preheated broiler until lightly browned, 2 to 5 minutes.

4 servings

Hot Crab

1 tablespoon butter
1 onion, minced
1 can (6½ oz)
  crabmeat, drained
Juice of ½ lemon
Worcestershire
  sauce
Salt and pepper
1 tablespoon fresh
  bread crumbs
1 tablespoon freshly
  grated Parmesan
  cheese

Melt the butter in a small skillet. Add the onion and cook, without browning, for 5 to 7 minutes. Remove and let cool.

Flake the crabmeat and remove any cartilage. Stir in the lemon juice; add Worcestershire, salt and pepper to taste. Add the onion and spoon the mixture into baking shells or ramekins. Sprinkle with the bread crumbs and the cheese.

Place the shells on a baking sheet and bake in a preheated 350° oven until heated through and golden brown, 15 to 20 minutes.

Garnish with parsley sprigs and lemon twists if desired.
2 servings

Grilled Sole with Shrimp Sauce

4 sole fillets
Juice of 1 lemon
2 tablespoons butter
SAUCE:
1 package (8 oz)
　frozen cooked and
　peeled shrimp
Grated rind and juice
　of 1 lemon
1 tablespoon
　chopped parsley
1 tablespoon
　chopped chives
Salt and pepper

Place the sole in a buttered broiling pan
and sprinkle with the lemon juice. Dot
the butter over the tops and cook under
a preheated broiler for 1 to 2 minutes
on each side. Keep warm.

Meanwhile, prepare the sauce.
Combine the shrimp, lemon rind,
lemon juice, parsley, chives and salt
and pepper to taste in a saucepan and
heat gently.

Roll up the sole fillets and arrange on
serving plates. Spoon the shrimp sauce
over; garnish with whole shrimp and
lemon slices if desired.

4 servings

43

Baked Trout

4 tablespoons butter
4 trout, cleaned
1 lemon, sliced
⅓ cup dry white
  wine
1 teaspoon dried
  tarragon
Salt and pepper

Line a baking dish with an extra-large piece of buttered foil. Place the trout on the foil and arrange the lemon slices on top.

Combine the wine, tarragon and salt and pepper and pour over the fish. Fold the foil over the fish to make a package and pinch to seal well. Bake in a preheated 350° oven for 30 minutes.

Arrange the fish on a serving platter and pour the juices over. Garnish with parsley sprigs and chopped parsley if desired.

4 servings

NOTE: Any non-oily fish may be substituted for the trout.

Summer Grilled Trout

4 trout, cleaned
Salt and pepper
1 tablespoon butter,
   softened
4 green onions,
   chopped
1 tablespoon
   chopped parsley
Juice of ½ lemon
4 dill sprigs

Season the trout with salt and pepper. Combine the butter, green onions, parsley, lemon juice and dill. Divide into 4 parts and stuff each fish cavity with one of the portions.

Place on a broiling pan and cook under a preheated broiler for 3 to 5 minutes on each side.

Arrange the fish on warm plates and serve at once. Garnish with dill sprigs and lemon wedges if desired.
4 servings

NOTE: Grilled trout is delicious garnished with slivered almonds. First brown the almonds lightly in butter, being careful not to burn them.

Salad Niçoise

8 anchovy fillets
3 to 4 tablespoons
  milk
¼ lb small green
  beans, trimmed
Pinch of nutmeg
½ small cucumber
Salt
½ lb tomatoes
4 hard-cooked eggs
2 cans (7 oz each)
  tuna, drained
8 to 12 pitted ripe
  olives
3 to 4 tablespoons
  French dressing

Soak the anchovy fillets in the milk for 15 minutes. Drain and discard the milk.

Cook the beans with the nutmeg in a pot of lightly salted boiling water until just tender, but still firm. Rinse under cold water and drain.

Cut the cucumber into sticks about half the size of the beans. Season lightly with salt.

Quarter the tomatoes and eggs and flake the fish. Arrange all the ingredients in a shallow serving dish and top with the French dressing.

4 servings

Danish Salad

4 hard-cooked eggs
1 green apple
1 red apple
4 pickled herring
  fillets
4 small potatoes,
  cooked and diced
⅔ cup sour cream or
  plain yogurt
Salt and pepper
4 pickled beets,
  diced
2 dill pickles, sliced

Slice the eggs, dice the apples and cut the herring into small pieces.

Mix the apples, herring, potatoes and sour cream together and season to taste with salt and pepper. Spoon the mixture into the center of a serving dish. Surround with the diced beets and arrange the sliced eggs and pickles decoratively around the edge of the dish. Sprinkle with chopped parsley if desired.

4 to 6 servings

Fettuccine with Four Cheeses

2 tablespoons oil
1 onion
2 cloves garlic
1 lb fettuccine
SAUCE:
2 tablespoons butter
2 cloves garlic, sliced
½ cup each grated
　Emmenthal, Bel
　Paese, Parmesan
　and Cheddar
　cheese
¾ cup heavy cream
Salt and pepper
Chopped parsley
Chopped basil

Add the oil, onion, garlic and pasta to a large pot of boiling salted water. Cook until the fettuccine is just tender but still firm to the bite.

Meanwhile, make the sauce. Melt the butter in a large skillet. Add the sliced garlic and cook, without browning, for 3 minutes. Stir in the cheeses and cream and cook, stirring over low heat, until the cheeses melt. Season with salt and pepper to taste.

Drain the pasta and discard the onion and garlic. Toss the pasta in the sauce, sprinkle with the herbs and serve hot. A tomato and onion salad would be a delicious and quick accompaniment to this dish.

4 servings

Pasta Mediterranean

3 tablespoons oil
2 cloves garlic, sliced
1 onion, sliced
1 can (16 oz)
　tomatoes
⅔ cup dry white
　wine
1 teaspoon oregano
1 teaspoon basil
1 tablespoon tomato
　paste
Salt and pepper
1 lb penne or
　macaroni
1 package (8 oz)
　frozen cooked and
　peeled shrimp
1 can (4 oz) mussels,
　drained
2 tablespoons
　chopped parsley

Heat 1 tablespoon of the oil in a large skillet. Add the garlic and onion and sauté, without browning, for 5 minutes. Add the tomatoes with their juice, the wine, herbs and tomato paste. Bring to a boil and cook, uncovered, until thick, 20 to 25 minutes. Season to taste with salt and pepper.

Meanwhile, bring a large pot of water to a boil; add 2 teaspoons salt and the remaining 2 tablespoons oil. Add the pasta and cook until just tender to the bite.

Add the shrimp and mussels to the sauce and cook gently for 5 minutes.

Drain the pasta and arrange on a warm serving dish. Spoon the sauce over the pasta. Sprinkle with the parsley if desired.

4 servings

NOTE: Cooked, shelled fresh mussels can be used.

Fettuccine with Cream and Mushroom Sauce

1 lb fettuccine
4 tablespoons butter
1 clove garlic,
   crushed
½ lb large
   mushrooms,
   sliced
½ cup heavy cream
Salt and pepper
2 egg yolks
Freshly grated
   Parmesan cheese

Cook the pasta in boiling salted water until just tender to the bite.

Meanwhile, melt the butter in a saucepan. Add the garlic and cook, without browning, for 1 minute. Add the mushrooms and sauté for 2 minutes. Add the cream and simmer for 10 minutes. Season with salt and pepper to taste. Remove the sauce from the heat and set aside for 2 minutes. Beat in the egg yolks.

Drain the pasta and add to the sauce; toss well. Serve at once, with Parmesan on the side.

6 servings

NOTE: You may stir some of the grated Parmesan into the sauced pasta before serving.

Spaghetti with Mussels

2 lb fresh mussels, rinsed (see note)
2 tablespoons olive oil
1 small onion, minced
2 to 3 cloves garlic, crushed
1 can (14 oz) tomatoes
3 tablespoons tomato paste
2 tablespoons dry white wine
2 tablespoons chopped parsley
1 teaspoon mixed dried herbs
Salt and pepper
¾ lb spaghetti
Freshly grated Parmesan cheese

Boil the mussels, covered, in a cup or two of water until the shells have opened, 5 to 10 minutes. Discard any that do not open. Shell the mussels and set aside.

Heat the oil in a saucepan. Add the onion and garlic and cook gently for 5 to 7 minutes. Stir in the tomatoes with their juice, the tomato paste and wine. Bring to a boil and add the parsley and mixed herbs. Season to taste with salt and pepper. Cook, uncovered, until thick, 25 to 30 minutes.

Meanwhile, cook the spaghetti in a large pot of boiling salted water until it is just tender to the bite. Drain.

Add the mussels to the sauce and heat gently. Toss the sauce with the spaghetti and serve at once, with Parmesan on the side.

4 to 6 servings

NOTE: Cultivated mussels need only a good rinsing before cooking.

VEGETABLES & SALADS

Bacon and Spinach Salad

2 tablespoons oil
4 slices bacon,
  chopped
1 onion, chopped
1 to 2 cloves garlic,
  crushed
1 lb fresh spinach
1 tablespoon lemon
  juice
Salt and pepper

Heat the oil in a large skillet. Add the bacon, onion and garlic and sauté for 5 minutes.

Add the spinach and lemon juice. Sauté for 3 to 5 minutes, stirring constantly, until the spinach is just tender. Add salt and pepper to taste and serve at once.
4 servings

Celery Hearts with Walnuts

1 lb celery hearts,
    quartered
2 tablespoons butter
¼ cup coarsely
    chopped walnuts

Place the celery hearts in a saucepan with water to cover. Cover and cook until tender, 6 to 7 minutes. Drain, place in a warm serving dish and keep warm.

Melt the butter in a small skillet and add the walnuts. Sauté until the nuts just begin to brown. Spoon the walnuts over the celery hearts and serve.

4 servings

Corn Fritters

1 can (12 oz) whole
   kernel corn,
   drained
2 teaspoons brown
   sugar
3 eggs, beaten
4 tablespoons butter,
   melted
¼ cup grated
   Parmesan cheese
Salt and pepper
Oil for deep frying

In a bowl, combine the corn, brown
sugar, eggs, melted butter, Parmesan
cheese and salt and pepper to taste.
Mix well.

Heat the oil in a deep fryer to 350°.
Drop the mixture by tablespoons into
the hot oil and fry until crisp and
golden, about 4 minutes.

Remove with a slotted spoon and
drain on paper towels. Keep warm
while preparing remaining fritters.
Serve warm, garnished with watercress if desired.

4 servings

Plain Omelet

2 or 3 eggs
Salt and pepper
1 tablespoon butter

Break the eggs into a bowl; add salt and pepper and beat lightly with a fork until well mixed but not frothy.

Melt the butter in an omelet pan until sizzling. Add the eggs and draw the mixture toward the center with a fork while tilting the pan to allow the uncooked egg to run out to the edges.

When the omelet is lightly browned underneath but still soft and creamy on top, tilt the pan and use a fork to fold about one-third of the omelet toward the center. Fold the other side over and turn the omelet onto a warmed plate. Serve immediately.

1 serving

Corned Beef Patties

1 can (12 oz) corned beef

1 can (16 oz) white potatoes, drained and finely diced

1 onion, minced

1 cup soft white or rye bread crumbs

2 tablespoons prepared horseradish, drained

2 tablespoons Dijon mustard

2 teaspoons Worcestershire sauce

2 eggs, beaten

Salt and pepper

2 tablespoons oil

In a bowl, break up the corned beef with a fork. Add the diced potatoes, onion, bread crumbs, horseradish, mustard and Worcestershire; stir to mix well. Add the eggs and stir to moisten throughout. Add salt and pepper to taste. Form into patties and chill for 15 to 20 minutes.

Heat the oil in a large skillet. Add as many patties as will fit in a single layer and cook until lightly browned, about 3 minutes on each side.

4 to 6 servings

Ham and Mushroom Suppertime Toast

1 package (1 oz) onion gravy mix
¾ lb mushrooms, sliced
1 cup diced cooked ham
½ cup sour cream or plain yogurt
4 slices white or whole wheat bread, toasted
2 tablespoons butter
Pepper

Prepare the gravy according to package directions. Add 1 cup water. Stir in the mushrooms and ham. Cover and simmer until the mushrooms are tender and the ham is heated through, about 5 minutes.

Remove from the heat and stir in the sour cream.

Spread the toast with the butter. Spoon the mushroom mixture over the toast and sprinkle with pepper to taste.

Serve at once, garnished with parsley sprigs if desired.

4 servings

NOTE: Any cooked meat can be substituted for the ham.

Cheese Rarebit

2 tablespoons butter
1 teaspoon dry
   mustard
½ lb sharp Cheddar
   cheese, shredded
3 to 4 tablespoons
   beer
Pinch of cayenne
   pepper
1 tablespoon
   chopped chives
Salt and pepper
6 slices hot toast,
   buttered

Melt the butter in a small saucepan
and stir in the mustard. Mix until
smooth and stir in the cheese, beer,
cayenne, chives and salt and pepper to
taste. Stir over low heat until the
cheese has melted and the mixture is
creamy.

Place the toast on a baking sheet and
spoon the cheese mixture over the
toast. Cook under a preheated broiler
for 1 to 2 minutes, until golden brown
and bubbling. Serve at once.

4 servings

Tomato and Cheese Open-Face Sandwich

4 slices whole wheat
    toast, buttered
4 large tomatoes,
    thickly sliced
Salt and pepper
4 basil sprigs,
    coarsely chopped
¼ lb sharp Cheddar
    cheese, shredded
4 slices bacon,
    halved

Place the toast on a baking sheet.
Arrange the tomatoes on the toast and
season with salt and pepper. Sprinkle
with the basil and cheese and top each
with 2 pieces of the bacon.

Cook under a preheated broiler until
the bacon is cooked and the cheese is
bubbling, 5 to 7 minutes. Serve at once.
4 servings

Pears en Compote

1 can (16 oz) pear
 halves
1¼ cups red wine
2 tablespoons butter
3 tablespoons
 crystallized ginger
¼ cup chopped
 walnuts (optional)
2 tablespoons Poire
 William (optional)

Drain the pears, reserving ⅔ cup of the
syrup. Combine the pears, pear syrup,
wine and butter in a saucepan and
bring to a boil. Reduce the heat, cover
and simmer for 10 minutes. Add the
ginger; combine well. Set aside to cool.

 Just before serving, add the nuts and
Poire William. Serve warm.

4 servings

NOTE: Fresh pears may be used instead
of the canned. Increase the wine to 1¾
cups and simmer for 20 minutes.

Baked Bananas

4 tablespoons butter
2 tablespoons brown sugar
2 tablespoons lemon juice
4 ripe bananas
2 tablespoons brandy

Combine the butter, sugar and lemon juice in a shallow baking dish. Cook in a preheated 350° oven until the butter is melted, 3 to 5 minutes. Stir well to mix the ingredients.

Cut the bananas lengthwise and on the diagonal into large pieces and add to the baking dish. Add the brandy, cover and return to the oven. Bake for 30 minutes.

Serve warm, with lightly whipped cream or over vanilla ice cream.

4 servings

Zabaglione with Macaroons

4 macaroons
4 egg yolks
⅓ cup sugar
¼ cup Marsala wine

Break the macaroons into small bits and divide equally among 4 dessert glasses.

Place the egg yolks in a bowl with the sugar and Marsala. Beat with an electric mixer on high speed over a pan of simmering water. Continue beating until the mixture becomes thick and mousselike.

Pour over the macaroon pieces and serve while the zabaglione is still warm.

4 servings

Orange Syllabub

Grated rind and juice of 2 oranges
Grated rind and juice of 1 lemon
2 tablespoons sugar
2 tablespoons Cointreau
1 cup heavy cream

Combine the grated rinds in a bowl with the juices and sugar. Add the Cointreau and let stand for 1 hour.

Beat the cream until soft peaks form. Beat in the liquid. Pour into dessert glasses and chill until serving time. Accompany with cookies if desired.
4 servings

INDEX